Better*Sweet*...

Rebuilding From the Inside Out

By Angela O. Bryce

Kingdom Journey Press
A Division of Kingdom Journey Enterprises
Woodbridge, VA

Table of Contents

Acknowledgements

I would like to express my love for my kids and husband, who inspire me to live life to the fullest, laugh often, and love unconditionally, and who demonstrate the true meaning of living life in the moment each and every day.

The sun beams down on my face and the sweat slowly trickles down my forehead. The Louisiana heat and humidity shine down on me as I peddle effortlessly on my strawberry shortcake bike. The seat is hot and my legs are sticky, but as I ride up and down the sidewalk, my only thoughts are on the frozen cup that I am going to get when my Granddad gets home. I love my Granddad so much. He stands tall, yet the biggest teddy bear! When he walks through the door, removes his hat, and settles down in his favorite chair, I will walk over and sit right on his knee and ask for a quarter for a frozen cup. My Granddad responds, "Were you a good girl today?" I laugh and say "Yes!" and like clockwork, my Granddad will slip me a quarter for a frozen cherry cup. Its moments like these that remind me of the joy, laughter, simplicity, and innocence of life and love. Its moments like these where I say to myself "Yes, I am good. Yes. I am joy. Yes. I am."

Introduction

How does a woman rebuild her life after tragedy, divorce, or simply after having made choices that neither serve nor promoted her total well-being?

Imagine waking up after 20 years of going through the motions of life, making decision after decision based on what others believe, think, or feel you should be doing, and then all of a sudden realize that you never really lived life, but have merely just gone through life with your eyes wired shut? Is it possible to reverse time and pick up at a point in your life when everything was picture perfect? Can you go back to a time and place where you did not have a care in the world, except maybe wondering if you would be allowed to play outside a little longer with your friends, or whether or not your parents would allow you to have ice cream after dinner?

Not so!

Life moves on and time does not stop or revert back for anyone.

I believe each and every one of us comes to a point in life where we think about the choices we made and the paths we have taken in life and then question whether or not we are truly living out our purpose, or simply going through the motions of life. I came to that point in my life seven years ago. I was in the middle of a divorce, broken, depleted, and questioning my value and worth as a human being. Seven years ago, sitting in the middle of my living room floor, I prayed that God would help me rebuild my spirit, mind, and soul. There was no turning back in time; however God did something much better. God began a work in my heart, mind, and soul.

This book is my story and testament of how God can take a broken, wounded soul, and transform it into a beautiful, loving, strong, gifted and uplifted being. This book serves as a guide to help you wherever you may be in the stage of rebuilding, and encourage and inspire you to move forward and move on.

This is my story of commitment to becoming better after having been broken for so many years, and to becoming a better woman who is already fully aware of what it means to be whole, free, and loved.

Remember, there is not anything that God cannot restore, transform, and rebuild, if we open up our hearts and allow Him to do so.

Preface

There comes a point in life where you find yourself at a crossroad. At this moment, you have a choice to either go right or left, and/or surrender to God's will and freely allow Him to mold you into the person He wants you to be. Better*Sweet* is my story, testimony, and journey of surrendering to God at my weakest moment, confronting all of the "stuff" and allowing God to heal those areas that were broken, and restoring me to a place of peace, joy, and love. You see, I had a choice, as we all do...to either let the past define who I was, or choose to be better, whole, and evolve into the woman God designed for me to be and who I am born to be. I chose to surrender and let God be God, and to allow the unconditional, undeniable love that He has for me to heal, restore, and rebuild me from the inside out. As you partake in my journey, my only request is that you be open and willing to allow God to mend any area of your heart, mind, and soul to a place of peace and restoration. Enjoy!

Much love,
Angela

And he said unto me, My grace is sufficient for you,
for My strength is made perfect in weakness...for
when I am weak, then I am strong.
2 Corinthians 12:9-10

Power and Strength Reside In Knowing Who You Are Today, and Forgiving All of the Past Yesterdays.
Angela Bryce

Chapter 1: My Life, Story, and Testimony

We all go through stages in life where we reach a crossroad and have to make a choice of whether to go right or left. There have been times in my life that I felt as though I was standing at the fork of the road, contemplating the journey to my left and cautious of the journey to my right. This book is my story and journey during those times, which ultimately led me to the path of wanting and desiring more for myself and my family.

In 1979, my parents were eager to move to a new city with better opportunities. My dad was accepted into Howard University's Medical School in Washington, DC, so my family packed up and moved from Louisiana to a city outside of Washington, DC in Virginia. Being a fairly close knit family, my mom's brothers and sisters soon followed suit.

On the weekends, my parents would often drop my siblings and me off at my aunt's house for a barbecue or to spend the weekend, while my parents went to school or if they had to work. My aunts would take my sister and me shopping on the weekends and spoil us with clothes and toys. My aunts were also infamous for hosting huge cookouts and throwing parties on the weekends, which made the weekend visits to their home more than enjoyable. The cookouts were always so much fun, yet in the midst of wonderful shopping sprees and tasty meals, my aunts would often discuss my parents and my mom's kids, which included me of course.

Did I mention, I was a little nosey, as a kid?

Well, I was.

Being a child and listening to grown-up conversations, I overheard some of my aunts talk about various topics, which included my mom and dad, some good, and some not-so good. The conversation would also turn to how my parents' children would turn out later in life. It was weird, and strange, having to overhear my family talk about my parents, and my sisters and brothers. It was even weirder to hear them discuss what they believed we would be or how much trouble we would give our parents as we got older.

Just imagine being eight years old and listening to your family talk about how you will be the one to get into trouble because you were shy or the quiet child. At the time, the conversations among my aunts seemed harmless, however it was still very uncomfortable to hear. To the ears of a young girl, hearing how you may or may not turn out from those closest to you and those whom you love can cause you to believe that their words may ring true. At the time, I was too young to ask myself the questions: "Is that true? Will I be the "black sheep"?" I was too young to formulate my own truth about who I was or who I would become, which later resulted in me making some life choices where for a number of years, I lived up to their expectations of being the "not so good" child.

All in all, I enjoyed hanging out with my extended family. To me, my mom's sisters were probably the coolest aunts in the entire world! As my sister and I got older and transitioned into our teenage years, it was our extended family of aunts who we turned to if we were in trouble or needed a shoulder to cry on. It was my Aunt Shelly and Uncle Marcus who took me into their home when my parents decided I needed a different environment away from the "bad" influences. It was then that I was introduced to a more structured environment with responsibility, which came after I rebelled against my parents because I wanted to live my way.

My Child, My Child

When I was growing up as a child, I was quiet and shy. My parents had four children; I was the middle kid and second to the oldest of four. I wasn't ignored that much, but since I was shy and overly sensitive, my family joked that I was either "up to something" or "scared". On the flip, I was the peacemaker and if anyone came to me with a secret or spilled their heart, they knew my mouth would be shut. I believed in loyalty and friendship, which I still take pride in to this day.

As with any other child, I enjoyed playing with my friends, running around outside, reading books, writing, singing, and listening to music. However, because I was reserved, my circle of friends was small.

When I was in elementary school, I remember the teacher calling me to the front of the classroom to answer a question. I recall sitting there, quiet as a mouse, pleading with my eyes to my teacher to allow me to remain in my seat and answer the question. My teacher, frustrated with my so called "in ability" to speak, encouraged my parents to have me tested for a learning disability. I met with a Special Education teacher who conducted a series of tests and then sent me back to the classroom.

Unable to find anything wrong with my mental abilities, except for my lack of desire to speak during class, the teacher decided that for a portion of class I would be sent to a class with children who had disabilities and needed special instruction. Thinking back to those days when I was a kid, I was somewhat relieved that I did not have to sit in class, but annoyed that I had to point at pictures and put together puzzles.

I remember sitting in this strange, small classroom with children who literally could not speak, and others who were wheelchair bound, and thinking that I could help some of the kids in the class, which I eventually ended up doing. I would help the other students with puzzles, games, and reading. Still, I remember feeling incredibly horrible and my self-esteem was shot. I remember sitting in the classroom one period helping a little girl with her snack, when my older sister's sixth grade class walked by the classroom. I heard one of the girls whisper, "Isn't that her little sister?" I remember going home and crying myself to sleep that night.

In the months that followed, the Special Education teacher requested that I be tested again and the school soon realized that not only did I NOT have a learning disability, but my language and reading skills were above average by more than two grade levels. So, they removed me from the special education class and placed me in an accelerated language arts and reading group. Go figure.

That experience stayed with me for a very long time. At that age, it seemed as if the entire world appeared to only focus on the fact that I had been placed in a Special Education class, as opposed to the final conclusion which revealed that I did not have a learning disability.

My spirit and self-esteem had been crushed. The damage had been done, and I believe it was during this time that I began to see myself a little differently than many other kids growing up around me.

As a child, I often daydreamed that I was in another place, different time, and a different person. If I was not singing along to a Diana Ross or Whitney Houston song, I had my nose in a book, or I was writing poetry or in my diary. Often times, I would pretend that I was an award winning actress and practice my acceptance speech on stage, which was actually our bathroom or bedroom! While my aloofness towards strangers and unfamiliar faces caused me to remain distant from many, my heart and mind however soared in my element or place of comfort. I suppose we all have a place inside of us that dreams of soaring and living that seems much unlike our own.

For me, it was a means of escape from the reality of my world of not being good enough or being "different". I began feeling more and more self-conscious about myself, and misunderstood by my parents and those around me. As I got into middle- and high-school, some of the kids from school often made fun of me because I was quiet, super skinny, smiled a lot, and spoke very proper. While many kids around me were perfecting their "coolness", I was busy trying to sound and act "hip". Do not get me wrong, I was not a "valley girl", but I was close to it!

I grew up in an area of Northern Virginia that was very diverse, and listened to nothing but old school R&B, hip-hop, and pop music. As a way of fitting in with the other kids in school, often times I would change the way I spoke to try and sound like the other kids, but it sounded so rehearsed and fake so I opted out. I was different, and yet I still wanted so badly to fit in.

Pushing The Limits

As I was growing up, I often felt stuck in between being a free spirit and being with the in-crowd. I often suffered silently, longing for something more in life. I experienced phases of depression that was masked with an appearance of shyness and sweet solitude for those whom I barely knew. I was however able to let go, be silly, and stretch boundaries with friends who were very close to me. Yet as I pushed the limits, there was only so far that I allowed myself to go with being outgoing and outspoken, or with taking risks and experimenting. Deep down inside, I had a strong conscious that would talk to me and tell me "slow down". I recall nights when I would kneel down beside my bed and ask God to cover and protect me.

When I was around thirteen years old, I my parents allowed me to spend the night at my best friend Mardea's house. Her parents were from Sierra Leone in Africa. Mardea, like me, had very strict parents, older siblings, and longed for adventure and a better life.

It just so happened that the weekend I was staying at Mardea's house, one of the biggest Go-Go bands in Washington, DC was going to be performing at the local Recreation Center. Go-Go music originated in Washington, DC and is a combination between R&B, hip-hop, and funk. Thousands upon thousands of individuals love the pulsating beats, heart-pounding drums, and call-response vocals of Go-Go Music.

Lisa and Mardea both fell in love with Go-Go Music. Mardea's parents agreed to allow Lisa to attend the party with cousins, and Mardea and I were allowed to go under Lisa's supervision. I was excited about going to my first Go-Go and was even more excited to be hanging with friends. The night before we left for the party, I read a passage from the Bible, Psalms 23. I remember feeling a bit nervous and reading passages from Psalms always seemed to calm my spirit.

The recreation center was packed! I had never seen so many teenagers and young adults in one place nodding their heads and moving to the music. People were laughing, dancing, singing, and drinking.

Mardea and I stood in amazement, taking in the "new world". Not only were we amazed at the scene, but we were thirteen, "boy crazy", and there were so many fine guys at the "Go-Go". Needless to say, I loved it!

Mardea and Lisa's cousins drove down from Maryland to attend the event and spotted us as soon as we walked through the door. As we made our way to the dance floor, I could not help but notice the way people moved on the dance floor. In one area, a group of girls were battling it out to see who could shake it the hardest. In another area, there were couples pulsating against one another and grinding to the beat of the music. Then there was me...

Did I mention Go-Go was not my favorite type of dancing music? I was on the dance floor rocking to the beat...barely moving my feet.

The music was loud, a bit too loud! Suddenly, the band started to switch up the beat to play "Doing the Butt". This was one song that I knew and one Go-Go song that I liked. Plus, "The Butt" was a dance that I could do! I started moving a little more and shaking my derrière, which is not that hard to do!! At this point, I love the scene and life. Then in almost a second, a very strange feeling came over me. I asked Mardea if she wanted to go to the bathroom and we proceeded off the dance floor. As we made our way to the bathroom, all of the sudden, we heard yelling and screaming, and there was a huge commotion on the dance floor.

A young lady screamed, "He has a gun!"

Mardea and I started running and headed for the door! In an instant, hundreds of other people started running out the door, knocking people over, attempting to escape the crossfire.

Imagine a scene from the movie *Bad Boys II* - guys with guns racing around the corner of the center. Mardea and I were glued against the side of the wall, unable to move and in fear of getting hit by a stray bullet.

My heart was racing and I was unable to move, scream, or even cry. Silent prayers of protection raced through my head. A plea for God's heavenly angels to lift me out of the madness screamed from every part of my being, but I could not speak.

As I turned to my right, my best friend was bawled over in fear, crying and looking just as terrified as I was. We were both shook, and to make matters worse, our ride Lisa – Mardea's older sister - was nowhere in sight.

Just as I begin to think that we may have to take a chance and run out into the madness, Lisa pulled up from around the corner and Mardea and I leaped into the car. Just as I jumped into the car, we heard shots. I looked down to my side and noticed a slight red blotch on the side of my waist. I screamed out "oh my God, I've been shot!" Then I looked down and noticed that a cup of juice had spilled on the seat. We all started laughing and crying simultaneously. We were happy to be alive, safe, and on our way home away from the madness.

As a teenager, I tested the limits. When pulled by the desire to step over the boundaries a little more, I was often overcome by a sense of caution. Later on in life, greater awareness brought to light how this sense of caution was only masking the underlying fear that I describe as being "overly cautious", thus causing me to begin taking risks and steps to become a better me.

Living in a home filled with high expectations and a strong emphasis on what was deemed acceptable and right, I had a difficult time accepting and loving myself completely as I was. I was skinny, with full lips and thin hair. When I looked in the mirror, I criticized everything from my eyes, smile, hair, and legs. I over analyzed every part of myself, inside and outside. In an effort to feel "normal", I rebelled against my parents, and in many ways I rebelled against myself.

When I was fourteen years old, I remember sneaking out of my parents' house with my best friend and going to a party at a guy's house that we knew from school. If you can imagine, there was plenty of alcohol and many kids drinking it.

When we got to his house, people were everywhere drinking, laughing, smoking, and partying. I remember sitting on the couch and looking around and thinking to myself, "Why am I here right now?" It was as if I was having an outer body experience where my eyes were traveling around the room and included looking directly at myself sitting on the couch. It was surreal. My conscious told me to get up and leave, but I just sat there taking it all in. That same night, or should I say morning, I got caught sneaking in the house. Needless to say, my parents beat my butt! I really could not be mad at them because I knew it was well deserved, and I was somewhat relieved.

When I entered my junior year of high school, my parents decided to move to Stafford, Virginia. It was by far one of the best things my parents could have ever done for me. I had an opportunity to start fresh. Sure, I was leaving behind all of my friends, my "first love", and what I knew to be familiar, but I had a chance to get out of my comfort zone and experience something new. It was around that time that I began to long for something more in life...

Up until that point in my life, my solstice was in my room for hours on end reading, writing in my journal, talking on the phone, singing, and earnestly longing for a change. There was something deep inside of me which longed for something more than just going with the flow of life. It was in that moment that I decided to start caring more about the direction and choices I was making in my life. I guess one could say that I was growing up or transforming, BUT, I was still a teenager, and teenagers are kind of "hard-headed"!

When my parents moved to Stafford, I quickly adapted to the small town feel, two lane roads, pick-up trucks, and "southern" Virginia swag. I became really good friends with a girl named Kendra who lived around the corner from me, and who was originally from Philadelphia. Kendra's mom was a single parent, and was very down to earth and easy to talk to. Kendra was pretty, smart, and she loved to talk, sing, and simply have fun! We instantly clicked, and became really good friends.

Kendra had just recently moved to Stafford the year before I moved to the area. Kendra had an older boyfriend in the military, and my boyfriend lived about 30 minutes away, so it was inevitable that we would not be friends! Plus, I was and have always been a great listener, intuitive, and trustworthy, and those qualities always seemed to shine through, so I never had issues with people wanting to be my friend. A stranger could easily stop me on the street and tell me their life story without the fear of the whole world knowing their business, which is one of the main reasons why we hit it off so well. At the same time, since we were both still young, I was not fully immersed in a total transformation. I wanted a new start, and we both enjoyed having a good time, which landed us in crazy predicaments.

I can recall a time when Kendra and I had gone out with a couple of our guys friends to a party where we had been drinking, and one of the guys started smoking a blunt, and passing it around. Instinctively, something told me not to smoke. However, I ignored it, and 15 to 30 minutes later, the room was literally spinning, everything, and everyone started moving in a slow motion, and I started to panic. I remember going home that night, and vowing to never put myself in that type of situation again. I remember waking up the next day, replaying the events of the night before and shaking my head because I clearly remember the little nudge or whisper saying "Not to do it", but I ignored the voice and the warning.

There are signs, clues, and warnings along the way about the choices we should make, paths to take, and ways to go, but it is up to us to adhere to those little voices, or hunches. If it is not for us, we will soon find out, or maybe it won't be for years down the road, but I believe those signs are there and they appear to help steer us in the direction that God has for us. As I said, I was still a little hard-headed, and free-spirited to want to adhere to those warnings at the time.

Have great hopes and dare to go all out for them.
Have great dreams and dare to live them. Have
tremendous expectations and believe in them.
Norman Vincent Peale

Family Ties

When I was growing up, my parents were very strict, especially with my older sister and me. I want to believe it was because we were girls and they were just being protective.

My dad, born and raised in Lagos, Nigeria, believed the best way to a better life and future was through education. My grandfather was a General in the Nigerian Army, and my grandmother was a feisty African Brazilian woman who believed in discipline beyond measure.

My father used to tell stories of how strict and downright mean my grandfather was and how very quiet and reserved my grandmother was when he was growing up. Once my family moved to Stafford, my father decided to bring my grandmother from Nigeria to come and live with us. It was only when my grandmother came to live with us that I could see she wanted the very best for her family. Her greatest desire was for her children, including her grandchildren, to be sound and rooted in God. In addition, I can only assume my grandmother's upbringing and childhood experiences caused her to be stricter than normal, and less lenient than many other parents growing up in our culture. Because my grandfather was high in the ranks of the Nigerian military, more than likely my grandmother wanted all of her kids to be on the path of the "straight and narrow" and not disgrace the family or its name.

Angela O. Bryce

Prior to meeting my grandmother for the first time, and based on my dad's description of her, I imagined her being heavy in weight, tall in stature, loud, and somewhat overbearing, however, my grandmother was quite the opposite. She was small in stature, barely 5'2" tall, walked very lightly on her toes, and her voice was high pitched and very soft. There was one keen feature of my grandmother that stood out most and that was her piercing gray eyes. My grandmother's eyes appeared to see through the core of my being.

From the moment, my grandmother and I met face to face, we connected. There was something about her demeanor and quiet strength that pulled me in and made me curious about her and the life she lived. It was during my grandmother's stay that I began to open my heart more and more to God and having a relationship with Him rather than "religion".

A well-known author, Stormie Omartian wrote a book called *The Power of a Praying Wife*, but prior to Stormie, there was the Power of a Praying Grandmother! My grandmother was the first person to ever express to me the importance of prayer, reading the Bible, and building an internal relationship with God. Morning, noon, and night, my grandmother would walk around the house holding her rosary and praying. She undoubtedly demonstrated "Prayer without ceasing".

I often sat with my grandmother, either in her bedroom or at the kitchen table, and listened to her pray. Her beautiful gray eyes would be looking out into the distance, and with tears streaming down her face, they were light but intense prayers to God that came from her that were so profound. Every so often as my grandmother would pray, she would blurt out the name of Jesus with such force. It was almost as if Jesus was standing in front of her. It was interesting to watch her with such fascination and intensity during her prayer sessions.

My grandmother was the first person to introduce me to the Psalms in the Bible. She told me that if I ever wanted protection, comfort, love, and guidance, I should read the book of Psalms, so I did. I fell in love with Psalms 121, and my favorite verses are 1-2 which says:

> *I will lift up my eyes unto the hills, from whence*
> *cometh my help. My help cometh from the lord,*
> *which made heaven and earth...* (KJVH)

Grandmother would often tell me how God can and will show you "MIGHTY" things if you pray!

Sometimes I would wake up in the middle of the night and hear the soft cries, not of pain, but of gratitude coming from my grandmother's bedroom. I would listen and often wonder what could make my grandmother so engrossed in prayer that she would not sleep or did not want to sleep. This connection she had with God amazed me and terrified me at the same time.

Often times, it seemed like my grandmother was the only person who knew truth and knew lies. Her spirit of discernment and intuition was beyond accurate; it was on point! For example, when I told my parents that I was going out with friends, my grandmother knew instantly that I was going out with my boyfriend. When I began contemplating going to school without even telling anyone, my grandmother stopped me in the hallway and said, "Yes, you are very sweet and will go to school and do great things, oh yes you will!" I knew it was her "access" and communion with God that kept her steadfast and "aware". Again, it was still frightening and amazing to be a witness to it.

My grandmother only stayed with us for two years and eventually went to live with my uncle. Shortly after moving, she passed away. I am forever thankful to have known her and shared the few years that I had with her before she passed away. It was during this period when I realized the importance of what having a relationship with God meant, and how this connection, even though it could not be seen, resides in us and all around us. It was during this period of my life that my perspective and outlook of God began to change, which made me more aware and sensitive to the voice of the Holy Spirit inside of me.

Being a young teenager at the time, the voice of temptation overpowered the voice of the Holy Spirit living inside of me, not to mention the voice of raging teenage hormones. Needless to say, being as young as I was, I was still wrestling with myself and trying to find my own voice.

Finding Your Voice

Are you familiar with the saying, "If you do not stand for something, you will fall for anything?" For years, society and the media have imposed standards on what women should be, look like, speak like, and sound like. Whenever we turn on the television, we are bombarded by images of women who weigh 115 pounds, wear a size 2, have perfect breasts, and have bodies that show no signs of bearing kids such as stretch marks or cellulite. It is no wonder many of our teenage girls have a complex about weight. For these reasons, a person has to know what they stand for and be able to speak and live their truth. Being able to look yourself in the mirror and love who you are because of the way you look, walk, talk, speak, laugh, cry, dance, and giggle are all a part of finding your voice.

I can remember as a child how I was terribly shy and would hardly speak in school or around strangers. Teachers would ask me questions in class, or demand that I go up to the board and answer a question or solve a problem. For some reason, I would be too shy to speak or walk up to the front of the class because in my mind, a little "critter" would whisper things such as, "They are going to make fun of the way you talk, or your legs are way too skinny, or your arms are too long". For a long time, I would suffer from a certain amount of anxiety when around strangers and individuals that I did not know well. Those voices haunted me in the company of close friends, but I felt comfortable enough to open up and be free around people I knew.

The people who were closest to me knew my love for singing and writing music. These were the only two outlets that I felt allowed me to freely express myself, however it took years for me to gird up the courage to sing in public.

On one occasion my Aunt Belinda, realizing that I had a beautiful singing voice, asked me to participate in a showcase to help raise funds for her church. I was excited to participate in the showcase and even more excited to be able to fulfill a dream of singing and performing. The thought of making a fool of myself and cracking up still haunted me though.

During each rehearsal I did not give my all because I was afraid of letting it all out. There was no doubt that I had and still have a beautiful voice, but I was holding back. After much deliberation, my aunts and I decided to perform a song by Janet Jackson called *I*

Get So Lonely. The fear and anxiety of messing up during the performance had me afraid of giving it my all.

During practice, I would sing my heart out, however each time it came to a point in the song where I could either play it safe or play with my voice and range, I would tense up and hold back. Finally, it was the night of the showcase and it was AMAZING. We gave our all during the performance and for the first time in many years, in a literal sense, I found my voice. I stood up, showed up, and found my voice of courage. And now many years later, I continue to write music and sing both on the inside and out.

What about you? Have you found your voice to stand up for what you believe to be true about yourself and your life? Or are you torn between what society has expected that you "should" do with your life? What do you believe about your values, beliefs, and morals that cause you to be willing to take a stand and take a step to be free with whom you are?

Find your voice of strength, courage, and peace on the inside, let it resonate within you, and let it speak loudly outside of you. The only person in the world who defines who you are is you.

ACTION STEP:
What does it mean to find your voice? Give an example of a personal experience where you were able to "find your voice". Describe how it made you feel.

_____

_____

_____

_____

_____

Dare To Dream...A Little

It would be unfair of me to not express all of the wonderful and amazing things that happened in my childhood. If it had not been for many of the things I went through, I would not be the person I am today. Yes, I was a shy child and had very low self-esteem, but deep down inside I knew that I wanted more for myself. There was a little voice inside of me though that had a hard time believing that I deserved it and that my dreams were possible.

During my junior year in high school, I decided to sign up for a Drama class as one of my electives. I thought it would be something fun, and an "easy A" to boost my GPA. I walked into the classroom on the first day of class, took one look at the Drama teacher and thought, "Well, this is going to be interesting".

Ms. G. was about 5'3" tall, had a thin build and long brunette hair, and was wearing baggy blue jeans, a white oversized shirt, and a colorful beret on top of her head. This may not seem at all strange to you, but it was more so her demeanor that stood out to me. Ms. G. was quirky, outgoing, expressive, and laughed ALOT. You must remember that back in high school when you had a teacher that let you chew gum in class, he or she was labeled "cool". Ms. G. was unique and she expected her students to be original and express themselves in ways that were considered outside of the norm.

At the beginning of class, we conducted "warm ups", which consisted of moving our bodies and face, making the craziest sounds, and stepping out of our comfort zone. It was great!

I remember Ms. G. pulling me aside and saying, "You have a light inside of you, so just let it go."

That same year, a group of my closest friends and I presented the first ever Black History Program for the entire school. We developed the program and recruited students and teachers to participate. Being that I was in Drama, I knew that I wanted to show off my "skills", so I volunteered to act and portray none other than the legendary Diana Ross of the Supremes! As soon as I hit the stage, it was MAGICAL (Yes, I am tooting my own horn ☺). Seriously, I had a blast and the teachers and students enjoyed the entire program.

After the program, Ms. G. pulled me aside and said, "YOU WERE AMAZING AND YOU RADIATED UP THERE!" Hearing those words made me feel so good on the inside. It validated something in me, but still deep down, there was that little voice that questioned whether I was really that good or just hearing words of flattery.

On the outside, you would have thought I was on top of the world. Instead of relishing in the moment though and believing that all my dreams could come true, I was dwelling on the little things.

It is during those defining moments in our lives where we can either choose to follow our dreams, or choose to listen to the ego, or "little voice", that raises doubt and fear that makes us hunker down and choose the lesser of the two. Over the course of years, it is these moments, due to fear of the unknown, that I chose to settle for the secure or the road of least resistance, rather than taking a leap of faith and awakening the light of creation that was inside of me.

Yeah Baby...College Here I Come!

Shortly after my grandmother left and during the early part of my senior year of high school, I decided I would attend the local community college and then later transfer to a four year university. In the fall of 1997 after a year at the local community college, I left to attend school in Petersburg, Virginia. I have to credit the inner workings of "prayer" and a desire for a better future that made me decide to take the plunge and go away to school.

It was at Virginia State University that I had my first real encounter with college life and I was far from impressed. The school itself was great and I enjoyed the diversity and culture of the school, however there was a part of me that felt a bit out of place. While many of the students were consumed with the partying, I was thinking about money for class, and getting a job.

Prior to leaving for school, I had become accustomed to providing for myself and making my own money. I had been working full time for a local internet provider doing their billing and customer service. When I decided to go away to school, I quit my job and mentally prepared myself to be a "college student". It never occurred to me that I would not have the same "luxury" of making my own money while away at school.

Once I was away at school, what I imagined would happen turned out to be a completely different story. It was an adjustment for me to have to rely solely on my parents. Quite frankly, when my parents sent me funds, it was not much, but to a "college student", every bit helps!

A couple of weeks after my arrival at school, I decided to get a job at a restaurant located near my school. At the time, freshmen were not allowed to bring cars to school, but I begged my parents to let me bring my car to school so I would have transportation to and from work after class. My parents reluctantly agreed, largely because they were tired of sending me money. For a little while, I felt more in control of my life, again. It was all good…so it seemed.

This Is A Joke…Right?

I was adapting to the college lifestyle - classes, parties, and working part-time. I had started seeing a guy named Jeff who was a little older than me, fun to be around and talk to, and I enjoyed his company. As our friendship grew closer, we started dating exclusively.

Jeff lived in my hometown, and prior to me going away to school, we were inseparable. After I went away to school, we primarily saw each other on the weekends, but we talked on the phone every day.

As I was adjusting to being away at school, and as my relationship with Jeff was progressing, I truly felt as if things were falling into place. That was until one morning I woke up feeling slightly different, a little queasy and a little off. Back then I was not into the mind, body, spirit connection, however, I was fully in tune with myself to know that something was not quite right with my body. Nonetheless, I showered, got dressed and left for class, hoping whatever queasiness I felt would subside as the day went on.

My first class that morning was English Literature with Ms. Brown. Ms. Brown was an amazing woman; she was graceful, poised, classy, and spoke with such distinction. As soon as I approached the door, the same nauseating feeling came back again.

Mrs. Brown looked at me and asked, "Angela, are you feeling okay?"

I replied, "Yes".

I slowly sat down at my desk, pulled out my planner, and looked at the calendar. Sure enough, my period was two days late!

As I sat there attempting to focus my vision and listen to my professor, the only word I heard was "period" and the only sight I saw was tears.

I had to get out of the classroom to find out what was going on and get my thoughts and nerves together. I gathered up my books, purse, and keys, and then darted out the classroom, murmuring to the professor that I had to leave because I was sick.

Back in my dorm room, I immediately opened up my planner again and double checked the last date of my period. I was "guess estimating" so I thought it may be best to wait for a day or two because after all, my "cycle" could just be re-adjusting itself (if there is such a thing).

Who was I kidding? My cycle always came on like clockwork. So, I got up and went to the drugstore and picked up two pregnancy tests.

When I got back to my dorm room, I went directly to the bathroom and took the first pregnancy test. Positive.

I immediately took the second pregnancy test. Positive.

As I lay in my bed, tears streaming down my face, I thought of how disgusted and disappointed I was in myself and how angry my parents would be once they found out I was pregnant.

My emotions were all over the place and I had no idea what to do. When I told my Jeff, he was supportive and understanding and suggested that we hold off on making any hasty decisions. You must understand, at the time, my relationship with God was growing but I was coming into my own, having God in certain areas of my life but not all of them. I was a babe in God's kingdom, and I did not know or understand that no mistake, choice, or circumstance could ever cause God to ever stop loving me, so I shut the Holy Spirit's voice out and made the decision to have an abortion.

The day of the procedure, I remember walking into the clinic and feeling completely numb. I recall three young ladies sitting in the waiting room and one young lady, no more than 13 years old was there with her mother. At that moment, what I was there to do hit me and I became even more aloof. As I sat there, still and numb, I kept telling myself over and over that "this was for the best". The very thought of a life growing inside of me was hard for me to fathom. "It was a cell", so I told myself.

After forty-five minutes, it was over. As I walked out of the clinic, I realized that a piece of me had died in there, causing me to feel an empty hollowness in my heart. I felt more alone than I had ever felt in my entire life.

Days, weeks, and months went by and I felt myself changing mentally, physically, emotionally, and spiritually. I began suffering from depression and could hardly bring myself to go to class or even socialize.

I cried all the time and could not even look at myself in the mirror. I remember waking up one night to a little voice calling out "Mommy". I thought I had officially lost my mind.

I called my mom and asked if I could return home. When my parents asked why I wanted to return home, I made up a lie and told them that VSU was not the school for me. Even though it was partially true, I could not fathom telling my parents the truth and breaking their heart.

My parents had no idea what happened and assumed that I was just having a difficult time adjusting to being away from home. The following semester, I returned home instead of going back to college. Instead of dealing with the abortion, depression, and turmoil, I suppressed it. In my mind, it was easier to suppress the shame, pain, and guilt rather than deal with it. I made myself believe that I needed a fresh start and I just needed to get my life back on track.

The following fall, I transferred to George Mason University in Fairfax, Virginia. My older sister and I decided to rent a two bedroom condominium in Alexandria, Virginia and move in together. It was great living with my sister. The area was full of young professionals, close to Washington, DC, active, and just what I needed to move beyond the painful past involving the abortion.

During my second semester of college at George Mason, Jeff and I called it quits. We realized that we were both just going through the motions of the relationship and we were growing apart. I was completely removed from the relationship and Jeff was "doing his thing". The break-up was inevitable. When we split, I dove into work and school. Very little time was spent pondering over the break-up and demons of my past. I was numb to it.

During my junior year of college, I received an offer to work as a consultant for one of the best private government contracting companies in the Washington, DC area. I was elated! My career and academic life were thriving and I felt like I was finally moving forward. Numb. It was during this time that I met, and fell in love with the man I would later marry, Mike. In addition, I became a member of one of the most prestigious African-American women sororities.

On the outside, my life was picture perfect, but the wounds of my past still remained…. Unresolved, broken, and still hurting.

Young, Naïve, & In Love...Lust...Love...

During my last semester of college, my relationship with Mike developed into one that became serious. Mike was a country boy at heart, charming, handsome, and very outgoing. Mike came from a wholesome, traditional family, similar to my own, except they were super religious. I often joked that he was a country boy with sex appeal.

Mike was well-known and loved by pretty much everybody, and also a great dad to his daughter from a previous relationship. When I was with him, there was no one else in the world that mattered, except for him. To Mike, I was the girl who had it all - great looks, personality, job, and a place of my own. I was the definition of the independent woman. There was one kicker though - Mike and I fought all the time.

During the course of our relationship, things started to change. Instead of feeling on top of the world, I started to feel isolated. All of my time was consumed by our relationship. My close friends attempted to talk to me because they noticed a change. Still, I was in "love".

I recall one afternoon when Mike and I attended a party with some of our friends from school. One of my friends pulled me to the side and said there were rumors about Mike being with one of my friends and sorority sisters, Desiree. At the time, I did not want to believe it. I confronted Mike about it, but he denied it. I called Desiree on the phone and simply asked if she and Mike had slept together. With hesitation, Desiree admitted that she and Mike did indeed sleep together and it was during a time when he and I had taken a break from one another. You would think I would have gotten the picture and called it quits with him, but I wanted to believe that Mike was my prince charming. I wanted the relationship to work so badly that I stayed with him anyway because I longed for the "fairy tale" relationship with a happy ending.

Have you ever longed for something so bad that you refuse to see the red flags waving, and sometimes screaming, right in front of your face? This was me, but I somehow convinced myself that the issues would eventually disappear and Mike would love and accept me for who I was without having the desire for other women or outside influences. Little did I know at the time, which became a valuable lesson that I later learned, is that it is impossible to love and accept someone else if a person has not first learned to love and accept themself.

After a year and a half, and multiple dramas later, I learned that I was pregnant. This time, I was in a different place that I like to call "fairy naïve land". In fairy naïve land, I believed that because I had it all together, a "great" career and a wonderful man in my life, that things would be different.

Mike and I got married and our son was born later on in the year.

Our son was the joy of my life and such a radiant light in our world.

Once I became a mother, my perspective about life changed. I had been given a gift and huge responsibility. I wanted nothing more than to be the best person I could be for myself, marriage, and family, however, things between Mike and I became extremely worse. We would argue about everything from money, kids, parenting, friends, family, and sex. Our fights got progressively worse and I began to feel the wound in my heart expand.

After giving birth to our son, I began to suffer from post-partum depression. I despised the way I looked, and I felt so much disgust for myself. I felt so alone inside, and suppressing my feelings just did not seem to work this time. When I looked in the mirror, I simply did not know who I was anymore. I threw myself into what I knew best, which was my job and being a good mother. The more I tried to please my husband, the more of "me" disappeared.

During our fifth year of marriage Mike and I had our second child, Moriah, who was the perfect little angel. She was and still is the happiest, most outgoing little girl anyone could ever meet.

The birth of our daughter was the happiest time of our marriage, yet it was also the toughest for us. Even though our family was expanding, our issues both individually and collectively ran so deep that sweeping them under the rug and wishing them away would not suffice this time.

A little while after our daughter was born, Mike and I separated and ultimately divorced.

Better*Sweet*

Chapter 2: Turning Point

*You are now at a **crossroads**. This is your opportunity to make the most important decision you will ever make. Forget your past. Who are you now? Who have you decided you really are now? Don't think about who you have been. Who are you now? Who have you decided to become? Make this decision consciously. Make it carefully. Make it powerfully.*
Anthony Robbins

Fork In The Road

I got married at the tender age of 23 and had my first child at the age of 24. By the time I was 28 years old, I was going through a very painful and heartbreaking divorce. At that point in my life I decided that enough was enough! Finally, I reached the point where I was going to truly let go and let God lead my life in the path that He wanted it to go.

I can vividly recall sitting on my living room floor praying and asking God to help me. God ever so lightly whispered in my ear, "I am here", and it was at the moment that I laid it all out and surrendered my heart and life over to Him. I knew I could not and would not make it if God was not leading the way. I was standing at the fork in the road; one road led to "same ole, same ole", and the other road led to "freedom, restoration, and healing". Which path would I choose?

> *Tidbit: If you are in the midst of a difficult situation, be still and listen for the voice of God. Listen for what He is calling and speaking in order to give you peace, comfort, and joy at this very moment.*

During my weakest and most vulnerable moment, therein lied the strength of God. It is in my most fragile state that God used me, and also uses us the most.

Why? I suppose it is because we are so weak, carnally and emotionally, that we long for spiritual food that will lift our spirits. I believe our spirits crave the love of God. When we suffer from trials and heartaches, our spirit grieves, and the Spirit of God which lives in us also grieves.

I remember going through my divorce and wondering if the pain that ached my heart would ever stop. Perhaps it was not just the pain of my divorce, but it was the pain of many years of suppressing the feelings and emotions that were not dealt with that hurt me the most. I recall being so utterly depressed and only having enough energy to conduct minor day to day activities. I had to write on sticky pads to remember to take a shower, brush my teeth, and even get up out of bed! I was mentally and physically drained. I was operating completely in my own strength, and longed for God's strength.

I remember, after what seemed like a dreadfully long day, lying in bed with aching muscles and tears flowing continuously down my face. I prayed that God would give me the strength to get through the pain, and that He would heal my heart and family. That night as I was falling asleep, I could feel God's loving arms around me. It was as if He said, "I am here".

The next morning, I felt a little different and stronger, but yet still fragile. It was at that time that I knew God was in the midst and carrying me every step of the way, and that everything would be alright. I decided to take God up on His offer to live and work through me and to rebuild my life for the better. So it began, a journey, of many sorts, to mental, emotional, and spiritual transformation.

First Things First

We must know that God is in the midst of every situation, and if we call on Him, He will give us strength and peace. We must see and know that God is the source in which our strength lies, and if we draw on Him, He will be there living, breathing, and equipping us with all the strength we need to survive any challenging trial or tribulation in our lives.

Take this journey for yourself through spiritual, mental, and physical transformation.

ACTION STEP:

I challenge you to spend five minutes for five nights sitting in a quiet place meditating on the strength and power of God. Remember, this is your journey to personal transformation.

Nature often holds up a mirror so we can see more clearly the ongoing processes of growth, renewal, and transformation in our lives.
Mary Ann Brusset – Quoteworld

Mirror, Mirror On The Wall

Going through a challenging or life-altering situation can make some people question their worth or value, or affect their self-esteem. Going through my divorce made me examine all the choices I made in my life.

I remember on one occasion looking in the mirror and wondering who the woman was staring back at me. I had no idea who I was and it hurt so bad inside. I majored in Psychology in undergrad, and although I was not a psychologist or licensed counselor, I knew that I had to love myself again, better yet love myself for the first time.

God desired to show me just how valuable and precious I was to Him. But first God showed me the areas that needed to be dealt with, confronted, resolved, and healed. For the first time in many years, God revealed deep rooted issues which dealt with low self-esteem, and feelings of unworthiness. In my heart, mind, and soul, I knew these issues had to be addressed in order for me to heal and move forward in my life. God began to reveal the crooked places in my life that I had tucked away, which included the abortion, unforgiveness, self-defeating thoughts, and limitations that haunted my mind.

During the darkest period of my life, God lifted me up and breathed life into me. I am a firm believer that when God breathes life into us, all that He ordains, plans, and blesses us with is to be used for goodness. When we deviate from our natural, gifted design and play small in life, we wind up on a path of mediocrity that sometimes causes us to make decisions and choices that can hurt and hinder us.

God can and will reveal the wonderful and precious thoughts that He has about you, but you have to be willing and open to hear from Him. God revealed all of the beautiful places in my life and heart that He desired to flourish, grow, and blossom.

I began to fill my mind with images of the life that I wanted to live and a better life for my children: a life filled with goodness, laughter, joy, peace, kindness, and most importantly, love for God, myself and for others. I began a personal journey of self-empowerment and transformation, examining every area of my life. Most importantly, it was a journey wrapped in healing and love.

As with any lesson and journey, it is a process that begins with becoming aware of where you are in life and the person you desire to become. My journey began at that moment and is still happening, and now I encourage you to begin the journey of rebuilding your life for a better you and a better life. You can do it!

Next, I want to take the opportunity to provide you with key steps on how to rebuild your life spiritually, mentally, emotionally, and physically, and share with you key areas which helped me and many others heal, rebuild, and love.

During your journey, you have a choice between being bitter or better. Choose to be better. It's your time, your journey, and your choice.

Recognize It's A Spiritual Thing

Wayne Dyer wrote a book called *A Spiritual Solution to Every Problem* and in it, he suggests that every crisis, situation, or problem can be resolved if we bring God into the solution. Many people, including myself, attempt to solve challenges on our own, when in fact God is the power that works in us and through us. Once we accept, acknowledge, and allow God's hand to move in us, we are able to see the light as well as move through the challenges we face in life.

It was not until I fully surrendered my cares, concerns, and worries over to God that I understood the Scripture which says:

> *Come to me all of you who are weary and*
> *burdened, and I will give you rest. Take my yoke*
> *upon you and learn from me for I am gentle and*
> *humble in heart, and you will find rest for your*
> *souls. For my yoke is easy and my burden is light.*
> Matthew 11:28-30

During my divorce, I was weighted down by worry, concern, and burdens. I was broken-hearted and concerned about my children, and burdened with finances and the reality of being a new single-parent. Every morning and every night before I went to sleep, I prayed that God would carry me and give me strength for each day. My daily meditation would involve envisioning God's loving arms wrapped around me and my children.

Many nights, my vision would consist of God's presence, love, and protection penetrating through me and my children. Divine love, peace, and strength is what I continuously felt each and every time I prayed and meditated on God's presence.

As you journey through the process of temporary challenges, turn to God as your source of strength. Rest in the assurance that a higher power, stronger than you, lives inside of you and is available and ready to carry you through. It is through God's spirit, love, and guidance that you will find the comfort you need to get through any circumstance and situation you may face in life.

Can you think of a time when God's presence soothed and strengthened you during a difficult period in your life? How did it make you feel?

_____

_____

_____

_____

_____

_____

_____

_____

_____

_____

_____

_____

_____

_____

_____

_____

_____

_____

_____

_____

_____

_____

Better*Sweet*

Chapter 3: The Power of Prayer

I cannot count how many times my soul would continually call on the name of God in the midst of a painful situation. In the midst of praise, my soul and heart would be so full of gratitude that all I could do was say "Thank you". Sometimes, all that prayer consists of are the words "Thank you".

Prayer is a means of communicating to a higher life force and being, which resides, lives, and breathes through us. Stormie Omartian's book, *Power of a Praying Wife*, is filled with powerful, uplifting, and encouraging prayers about marriage, husbands, and the significant impact prayer has on a relationship.

Countless books have been written on the power of prayer for our health, healing, restoration, deliverance, families, peace, and love for ourselves and others. Webster's dictionary defines prayer as "a spiritual communion with God". Many people have given testimonies of the countless miracles that occur after prayer and even in the midst of prayer. When we go to God, Who lives in our inner most being, heart, spirit, and soul, we commune with a higher essence Who is intertwined with the core of our being. When we communicate with God, He intimately wraps His loving presence around us and softly whispers words of encouragement in our ears.

In your time of need, take time to speak to God and share with God all your thoughts, cares, fears, and deepest desires.

I vividly remember being in the seventh grade and experiencing the power of prayer and God's divine protection in my life. As I mentioned earlier, while I was growing up, I was often teased by kids in school about the way I looked or talked. There were many nights that I prayed to God to protect me, and He did.

I remember nights that I would come home from school, lock myself up in my bedroom, turn up the music, and cry myself to sleep. One particular night in the midst of crying myself to sleep, I opened up my Bible and murmured three little words - "Protect me God". With each word, my nerves subsided and calmness came over me.

If you ever wondered if God hears or if God is listening, know that He is always listening and He always answers us. The question is whether or not we are listening to Him.

Prayers spoken in your heart and mind have great power to resonate, shake up, and release change into the atmosphere. As we pray, change takes place in the invisible realm that may not be visible to the naked eye, but issues are being resolved on a spiritual level. With this change, your soul is being healed, which ultimately effects how we see ourselves and those around us.

ACTION STEP:
For the next 21 days, before you go to sleep and before you begin your day, take a deep breath and repeat the following prayer:

> _Dear God, thank you for today and thank you for renewing my mind, body, and spirit._

How Do You Feel When You Pray?

_____

_____

_____

_____

_____

_____

_____

_____

_____

_____

_____

_____

_____

_____

_____

_____

_____

_____

_____

The Mind, Mind, Mind

How do you keep from making the same choices and mistakes of the past? How do you pick up the pieces when so many areas of your life seem to weigh you down?

You may be weighed down with debt, mending a broken heart, in a difficult relationship, or suffering from the loss of a loved one or a terminal illness. How do you quiet the voices in your head that seem to scream at you and tell you that the madness will never end, or that you will never heal, get out of debt, or rebuild your life for the better? These voices prey on your ego and will mask themselves and have you believing you will never move from the feeling of despair. This is a lie!

One saying that always holds true is "This Too Shall Pass". The negative tapes that run in your head play a huge factor in how you perceive life, finances, relationships, and most importantly yourself. Our thoughts go a long way and what you believe about yourself can have a significant impact on who you believe you are.

In order to heal and see yourself in a different light, you must reprogram your mind with truth which speaks love, light, and goodness. You have to reprogram those negative thoughts and replace them with thoughts of goodness, joy, worthiness, healing, joy, peace, and love.

In order to truly rebuild, transform, and heal, you must be consciously aware of the thoughts you allow to go into your mind and how those thoughts affect your perception and reality. The work of Byron Tracy© is a tool and is described as questioning the thoughts which cause turmoil, fear, and disruption in our minds. For example, if you are contemplating accepting a new promotion, a new little voice in your head may say, "You will not succeed at the job." Instead of believing the thought, simply question whether or not the thought is true.

One of the biggest challenges and obstacles people face in moving forward in their life comes from within. The self-defeating negative voices will kick you even harder when you are down, and subconsciously, you may respond by making a choice, or choices, that support the "lies" that your ego and "little critters" (negative thoughts) have told you. If you desire to rebuild your life for the better, you need to recognize those voices and replace the self-defeating voices with thoughts that encourage and uplift you.

So how do you do that? Let me share with you how I did it and continue to do it today. First and foremost, I had to become fully aware of the thoughts that were playing in my head. They were thoughts like: "How are you going to make it? You're not good enough." Or, "How can I pick myself up out of this detriment and move forward? "

One day, I met with my therapist (I must repeat, therapy is good!), and she conducted a relaxation, hypnosis exercise. She instructed me to put all of my positive traits and attributes on an index card along with my favorite scriptures and bring them with me to my next session.

During the session, she guided me through a deep relaxation exercise, and during that process, she repeated all of my positive attributes and scriptures. I remember lying on the couch, drifting in and out of consciousness, present but not really present, and feeling light as a feather.

After the exercise, I felt peaceful and requested that we continue to do the exercise. My therapist suggested however that I take the recording of the relaxation session with me and listen to it every night before I went to sleep to begin the process of reprogramming my mind. That night, I went home and not only did I listen to the recording, but I made about 50 other small index cards full of affirmations and scriptures of blessings and goodness over my life and my kids' lives.

I knew I had to do something to change my life around. I knew that changing my life was not going to come from the world, but it was going to come from me. This single step started me on a journey of changing the way I thought of and saw myself as a spiritual being.

Reprogramming your mind will not happen overnight, but it will happen. It may take time for you to change the way you see yourself and to replace the negative thoughts in your mind with positive thoughts, but be open, willing, and determined to see yourself in the very best light because you deserve the very best that life has to offer.

MIND ACTION STEPS:
If you can replace one negative thought with an uplifting thought each and every day, you will be well on your way to changing the way you think about yourself. Here are some key steps that will help you in the process of changing your thoughts:

1. Guard Your Mind. Like a mother protects her newborn baby, you must guard and protect your mind. Screen everything that you see and hear. Years ago, I would sleep with the television on and the next morning I would wake up restless and cranky, unaware that my subconscious mind was soaking in all of the media from the night before. Once I started turning the television off at night, I noticed a major difference in my sleeping patterns and how refreshed I felt in the morning. You must screen everything you see, hear, and feel, and manage the information that you allow to enter your mind. Allow only positive information to enter your body. Proverbs 4:23 says, *"Guard Your Heart, For it is a Well Spring of Life"*. Guard what enters your spirit and eliminate information that is negative, defeating, and violent. If it means stop watching the news, violent shows or movies, and limiting the amount of time you spend with negative people and relatives, then take the necessary steps and actions to do so.

2. Sweet Self Talk – Spend time every day in front of the mirror and say something nice about yourself. This may seem corny, but it works! Compliment yourself on how great you look (even if you are just waking up!). I wake up every morning, look in the mirror and say "I love me!" Crust may be on the side of my eyes, and drool on the side of my mouth, but I still say it because I do love me and this is what I need to do in order to reinforce my mind and spirit that "Yes, I love me and care about who I am." Throughout the day, take some time and remind yourself of how beautiful you are and how *"you are fearfully and wonderfully made in the image of God"* Psalm 139:14. If God said it, then you know it is the truth!

Better*Sweet*

Chapter 4: Change Is For Sure

A Moment of Truth

One Saturday afternoon as I was picking up things off the floor, I could not help but to feel a nagging in the pit of my stomach. I looked up and my eyes stared intensely at one of the words on my vision board – SUCCESS.

Immediately afterwards, there was that feeling again in the pit of my stomach and this time a still voice inside which said to me, "You are worthy of success." I sat down on my bed, closed my eyes, and with everything in me, I repeated it again out loud, "I want to be successful."

My mind, soul, and spirit were longing to feel worthy of success, but for so long, I did not feel worthy. As I sat on the bed in my bedroom, closed my eyes and envisioned my life filled with happiness, laughter, love, and joy, my heart filled up with so much love that tears just began to flow down my face. This was a turning point and moment of truth where my thoughts and spirit were in tune. For me, it was a moment of clarity, truth, and belief that I was capable of becoming the woman I wanted to be and worthy of success and every good free-flowing blessing that God had for me and my family.

When will it be the turning point for you? Or has it come?

Reprogramming your mind and thoughts with uplifting, encouraging thoughts may not happen overnight, but if you can replace one negative thought with an uplifting thought each and every day, you will be well on your way to seeing yourself in a positive light.

ACTION STEPS:

1. On a 3x5 note card, write two affirmations that encourage and uplift you.

2. Repeat these affirmations in front of a mirror every night and every morning for 21 days.

_____

_____

_____

_____

_____

_____

_____

A Little Time With You...

For me, one of the most precious times of the day is early in the morning when the house is completely quiet, the kids are still asleep, and the sun is slowly rising. It is during this time that I mentally and spiritually prepare for the day, and that I pray, meditate, and write in my journal. I cherish the time when I have more than one hour or a couple of days to myself to reflect, work out, write, and simply enjoy being.

One summer while the kids were away visiting their dad, I decided to tackle one of my biggest fears. I was terrified of water, well not "water" but of being underwater. I remember taking a shower and washing my face only to hold my breath as the water hit my face. Granted it felt good, but something inside of me, "the little critters" in my head, made me feel as if I would drown.

Logical? ABSOLUTELY NOT!

I decided now was the time to face my fears and learn how to swim, so I registered for an adult beginners swim class. And guess what? I conquered my fear of the water and learned how to swim! I took advantage of the time I had alone to learn something new and conquer a fear that had me bound for years. In addition, I was able to get in touch with me and learn something exciting and new about me, which is priceless!

If you are serious about rebuilding your life for the better, spending time alone is essential and should be incorporated into your daily living. Quality time by yourself for just an hour a day will give you an opportunity to reflect on the day and your thoughts, particularly if you are going through a painful season in your life. Time alone will give you permission to deal with any feelings of sadness, frustration, and hurt that you may be feeling. In addition, quality "me" time gives you a chance to just be in the present moment and plan a better future for yourself.

ACTION STEPS:
Spend 15 to 30 minutes a day completely by yourself.
Here are some ideas to help you get started on how to spend quality "me" time:
- Go for a nature walk
- Read a book
- Pray
- Learn a new skill or hobby

The time you spend alone will help you clear your head and calm your mind. Time well spent is invaluable.

Repeat After Me.."Therapy Is Good"!

*Being in **therapy** is great. I spend an hour just talking about myself. It's kind of like being the guy on a date.*
Caroline Rhea

A survey published by the New York Psychotherapy Group from - Consumer Reports, November, 1995 concluded that therapy for mental health problems can have a substantial effect and improve the overall mental-health of individuals. Having majored in Psychology in college and being an advocate for therapy, I wholeheartedly agree with the findings and can fully relate to therapy improving the overall mental state of individuals. Knowing first-hand how beneficial therapy is to releasing and expressing pinned up feelings and emotions, a Therapist can assist you in dealing with the emotional ramifications of a loss, challenge, or divorce. Talking with a therapist will give you a chance to face the issues that not only plagued your situation, but address issues that you have inside from past hurts that have not been resolved. A counselor can help you forgive and move on in your life.

During my divorce, I saw a therapist every other week for nearly eight months and participated in a divorce care support group. I recall telling my mother that I was going to a therapist and to no surprise, she thought that seeing a therapist was "unnecessary". In her eyes, therapy was only for individuals who needed psychological "help". Well, one thing that I knew for sure was I needed to address my underlying issues and needed someone unbiased to talk to, therefore I needed help! I needed help in figuring why I had made so many decisions that caused me so much grief and heartache. I needed to understand my need to "please" or be accepted by someone who did not accept me. I wanted to know why I did not love and accept myself exactly as I was.

My counseling sessions were an opportunity for me to talk about all of my fears, anxieties, and worries that concerned myself, my kids, and my life. The therapist helped me address and confront the issues in my marriage, issues that I had with myself, and face reality as it stood during that moment in order for me to forgive and renew my life as a single person. As an individual rebuilding your life for the better, you want to have a safe haven to process emotions, and work through the process of healing to move on with life. A therapist will be able to assist you with that.

If you are not completely ready to see a therapist, then try a spiritual retreat or support group. I had always respected the work of many Self-Help Spiritual Teachers like Marianne Williamson, Louis Hay, Dr. Wayne Dyer, and Dr. Iyanla Vanzant. One year, while I was consulting in Maryland, I decided to attend a workshop on "Change" hosted by Inner Visions Institute and facilitated by Dr. Iyanla Vanzant. The workshop proved to be one of the most powerful investments I made in and for myself. It was during this time that I learned the importance of taking ownership and responsibility for my inner self, and reclaiming the power that lies within me. In addition, it was wonderful to be around so many like-minded women who were reclaiming and embracing change in their lives, minds, and spirits. Being with yourself and spending time getting to know who you are and the many facets of the "REAL" you is worth taking time out to explore.

Nothing Like A Strong Support System

Having a strong support system of individuals that you trust and who will be there for you during your time of rebuilding is priceless. There is nothing like having a strong support system of friends and family when you are in the process of rebuilding your life after a divorce or unexpected challenge. The pivotal point in my life occurred as I was going through my divorce and I made the conscious decision to rebuild my life for the better. Thankfully, my family, church support group, and close friends were there for me when I was down or wanted a shoulder to cry on.

A vital part of healing involved spending time with close family and friends that truly supported, and still support, my efforts to transform my life. I gained confidence and encouragement that I needed to get through periods of discouragement. My family, support group, and close friends were truly a blessing and continue to serve as one of the best support circles for me.

In the process of rebuilding your life for the better, one of the best things you can do for yourself is to surround yourself with a very strong network of loving friends and family. My sisters, by blood and friendship, served as that strong support group. Words simply cannot express how much I love and appreciate the bond my sisters and I share with one another. My sisters and I have been there for each other during the good, bad, and ugly.

I can recall on a number of occasions how my older sister, Nailah, called me at just the right time when I needed a shoulder to cry on, vent, or just simply talk to a "sane" person. Having a strong and honest relationship with my sisters provided me with the opportunity to share my concerns with individuals I trusted and who would not talk about or judge me.

My older sister, blessed with beauty and brains, has always been the one to "cut to the chase". She always emphasized the importance of taking a moment to "get it out and then move forward with a plan". I can vividly recall my older sister telling me straight up, that instead of complaining about certain situations, I needed to do something about it, whether it was my job, relationship, marriage, finances, etc. She told me I needed to create a plan, and move forward with it. It is no wonder that my older sister is extremely meticulous, a huge saver, and extremely organized.

My younger sister, Christina, has always been the most giving person in the world and has a keen sense for fashion and working out. She has always been someone who I could truly depend on and be adventurous with. I remember dragging my younger sister with me when I wanted to try my hand at rock climbing. Christina was there with a helmet and stilettos ready to give it a try!

Others in my family also served as a strong support system for me. At the time of my divorce, my parents lived out of the state, but never hesitated to visit or call to check on me and the kids. My aunts were also there to support me during this process. My family could tell that I was hurting and they knew my goal was to heal and create a better environment and life for the kids.

In addition to blood born sisters and family, my support group also consisted of close friends who only had the best intentions for their life and my life combined. First there was Nancy, a mom, registered nurse, and prayer warrior. There was Natalie, a divorced, single-mom, and true minister of God with a spirit to encourage, who found love a second time around. Then there was Stacy, my sorority sister, sister in Christ, true woman of strength, who always knew how to shift the focus to something positive.

There was Janice, my sorority sister and best friend, who is a secretly wild at heart woman! Then Ashley, a beautiful friend who literally knows how to brighten up the room with just her presence and beautiful smile! Last, but not least, Kara. Kara was the first person that held my hand at the very beginning of the process when I made the choice to rebuild my life for the better, and Kara was also the one who facilitated the events of my divorce party (those details will remain unwritten)!

Another important step in rebuilding for me was becoming a member of a divorce care support group. Every Wednesday for 13 weeks, I was able to share my feelings, grieve, vocalize, and process my emotions. I was not judged, but accepted unconditionally.

My support group was an outlet for me to surrender and release my frustrations and anger. We discussed the Bible and God's view of divorce and how it hurts God just as much as it hurts us, but how God forgives and wipes the slate clean for us. I was able to confront and face many of the issues that I ran away from in my marriage, therefore I was able to see and accept my role in the failure of my marriage. Most importantly, my divorce care support group gave me permission to deal with forgiveness of myself and my ex-husband on my terms.

Many people seek out other relationships and lovers to heal their wounds or broken heart, but I knew that opening the door to another lover or "friend" with benefits would only deepen the wound.

You may be thinking "What if I do not have a very supportive family and many of my friends are stagnant". If this is the case, then I highly recommend that you develop friendships with individuals who also desire to rebuild their life, or are where you would like to be in life. Doing so will allow you to be encouraged and surrounded by people who want nothing but the very best for you and celebrate each step that you take and milestone that make in your life. I highly recommend seeking out a support group to help deal with the pain and heartache, and embrace your new life fully, complete, and whole.

Face Time

If you can stand in front of a mirror, look yourself in the eye, and embrace the full you, imperfections and all, then I would say that you are on your way to complete and total healing. However, if you can only stand in the mirror and painfully gaze upon the person staring back at you, then you have some work to do in your life.

By facing the reality of what is going on in your life, you will be able to receive healing in your life and move forward. It takes tremendous courage to acknowledge and face the mistakes and messed up choices that you have made in life, and your broken spirit and heart. I am here to tell you that confronting the demons of your past will undoubtedly heal the wound in your heart and open the door to the freedom that you so deeply long for and deserve as a divine human being.

I can recall facing every demon that lurked in my closet mind and standing in the front of the mirror appalled at who was staring back at me. At 28, I felt like my life was in shambles. I had two small children, separated, and unsure of how I was going to take care of myself and family. I did not know which way was up or down, however I knew that I had to make some adjustments in my life and in order to do so, I had to deal with my issues. I had to fully understand how I got to that point in my life and why I felt worthless, unworthy, and unloved.

First, I had to ask myself some deep, intimate questions about who I was at that moment in my life. Was I as disfigured as I thought myself to be? Was I really to blame for all the mess in my life? I had to ask myself these questions and I had to answer them.

In order to answer these questions, I had to be honest with myself. I had to look inside myself for those answers. There was no running to hide or picking up a phone to call a friend who would boost my confidence and tell me what I wanted to hear. No, it was all on me. I was the only person who could provide the answers.

As with you, you are the only person who can answer the intimate questions that are permeating your soul. Why do you keep going around in circles? Why is it that you feel so under-valued? When you begin to ask and answer these questions and face the issues surrounding your life, will you be able to confront and master the art of overcoming those very demons that once had you bound.

It would be an understatement, to say the least, if I wrote that I had few flaws because I realized my issues with low self-esteem were deep rooted. I examined every area of my life and looked at where I went wrong and what needed to be adjusted. I realized that it all started from inside of me. I could no longer mask the pain and hurt that was inside because now the bloody beast was exposing its head and spilling over into every area of my life, including my children. Once I began to really and truly see myself, embrace my "stuff", and take ownership for my life did I begin to heal and restore my heart, mind, body, and soul. Believe me, if I can do it, anyone can do it. Begin today.

ACTION STEP:

Stand in front of the mirror for one minute and look deep into the eyes of your soul. What thoughts come up? Are you at peace with who you see? Do you want to cry? Are you haunted by the thoughts of past mistakes?

_____

_____

_____

_____

_____

_____

_____

_____

Worthy You Are and Always Have Been

There is a beautiful gospel song which sings praises to God on how wonderful, mighty, and worthy He is. The song reminds me of how mysteriously amazing God is and was to create us in His image and dwell in and among us.

Take a moment and assess how you view yourself when you look in the mirror. Do you see the perfect being God has created you to be? Do you see the beautiful being staring back at you, or do you only see mistakes that you have made? Are demons from your past weighing you down? Do you see yourself as worthy to be loved, adored, respected, and smothered with God's goodness, blessings, and mercy?

You are not alone if you answered anything other than Yes.

Unfortunately, there are a lot of women who do not see themselves as worthy. Seeing yourself as a valuable, worthy being means that you regard yourself with high esteem and you value who you are as a human being. Too often, women allow past mistakes to define their level of worthiness, which should not be the case. We must remember that to let go and forgive means to move on and realize that our worthiness is not based on what we did or did not do. It is based on knowing and believing you are a divine child of God, simply because you are. That is it. Remind yourself that to simply be is justification enough to know that you are worthy.

Move Something and Shake Something!!

Studies have shown that exercise not only helps you lose weight, but exercise also reduces stress, depression, and makes you feel better! When we engage in certain activities such as running, walking, and weight lifting, our body releases endorphins which are known as the "feel good" chemicals that enhances your mood.

I am a firm believer in exercise, yoga, and any type of movement which gets the blood pumping. When I think back to when I was a teenager though, I absolutely hated P.E.! The very thought of running a lap around the gym caused my stomach to turn and churn.

I remember being in high school and receiving a "D" in P.E. simply because I did not want to run the mile or bust a sweat and mess up my hair. Now years later, I cannot go two days without working out, Yoga, or engaging in some form of physical exercise. To me, exercise is another form of therapy. I can work out and release all of the cares of the day behind, work through issues, repeat affirmations, and just simply be. With exercise, I can get fit, healthy, and energized. It truly is a Win-Win.

On a much deeper level, working out helps me release much of the stress from the day, re-focus, and energize my mind and body, all at the same time. For individuals who are not accustomed to working out every day, or who do not belong to a fitness club, simple power walks around the neighborhood can rejuvenate the body or dancing around your house will get the blood circulating and juices flowing. Not to mention, it gets the happy hormones flowing in you!

In an earlier chapter, I talk about the importance of a strong support group. One of the best relationships and bonds I developed while going through my divorce was with my sisters, Nailah and Tina, as well as two instructors at my fitness club, Deitra and Camm. Both women had gone through similar situations and served as a living inspiration and witness that rebuilding, restoration, and healing were possible for me to move forward in life.

One of the fondest memories I have is when I started teaching Bodyflow at Elements Diet and Fitness Women's Club. In order to complete the certification process, I had to tape one of my classes and submit the video for a complete evaluation, assessment, and certification. Deitra and Camm took me under their wing and taught me the basics of engaging class participants, and awareness during each pose. During the process of providing great techniques, Deitra and Camm shared life lessons about being a woman comfortable in her own skin, excellence, and remembering to enjoy life no matter the circumstance. For me, this in and of itself was a step out of my comfort zone, however it was and still is motivating and inspiring to take steps to improve not only my body, but my health, and becoming fully comfortable in who I am as an individual and woman.

As a woman, you owe it to yourself to take care of yourself mentally, spiritually, and physically. Surrounding yourself with individuals who truly love and support you in all capacities in life will encourage you and motivate you to love yourself enough to step out of your comfort zone, confront fears, and rebuild your life for the better!

ACTION STEPS:
Challenge Yourself and Move with Movement Exercises
Day 1: Take A Brisk Walk For 15 Minutes – Nature Walk, Neighborhood, Park (Low Stress Places)
Day 2: Go To The Gym and Power Walk on the treadmill for 15 Minutes
Day 3: Turn Up the Volume to Your Favorite Song and DANCE! (So Much Fun and even Better when You and Your Family Join In On the workout!)
Day 4: Try 30 Minutes of Yoga

A Single Step Is All It Takes

When you wake up in the morning and look out at the sky, do you see the day filled with endless opportunities, or do you dread the day to come and see it as just another day to get through?

Many people make a determination on how their day is going to turn out by the number of clouds in the sky, or whether it's sunny, raining, or snowing! Well, I am here to say that each day that you rise and get out of bed is a gift that is to be unwrapped and opened up. Your life is a gift full of blessings, love, and grace, so cherish it.

It is so very important for you to see each day as a new beginning and a fresh new start. There may be days when you feel like staying in bed with the covers over your head, but when that happens, look up at the sky, take a deep breath and say to yourself,

"Today is a new day", and then move forward with one foot in front of the other.

I am a firm believer that God can and will give you the strength and courage to make it through any and every obstacle in your life, if you let Him. He lives and breathes in you. You live and breathe in Him, so allow the power that He has deposited in your soul to move through you and work miracles in your life.

Some people say the best time to deal with issues or problems is exactly when you do not want to confront them. I tend to have to calm myself down, breathe, take a step back, assess the situation, and then move forward by refocusing my energy on what truly matters in life.

James 1:12 says:

> *Blessed is the man who perseveres under trial,*
> *because he has stood the test, he will receive the*
> *crown of life that God has promised to those who*
> *love Him.*

You Are Me & I Am You

Any trial or test in life is an opportunity to heal, learn, and help someone else. I did not fully understand that until I went through my divorce, which had a tremendous impact not only on me, but also on our kids. At the time, my step-daughter was in 2nd grade, my son was in kindergarten, and my youngest was merely eight months old. It would definitely be an understatement to say that my plate was full. At that time, I became close friends with another mother in the school's carpool program named Anita. Anita defined "sister in Christ" because during the times when I wanted to give up, she was there to encourage and pray with and for me, especially when my prayers consisted of sobs. Most importantly, Anita had gone through a divorce and knew what I was going through.

There were many times when I would pull up to Anita's house smiling, yet masking the pain inside. She knew I had been crying though. I remember one day sitting at her dining room table and she leaned over and told me that I did not have to hold it in; if I wanted to be angry, I was allowed to be angry. I went home that evening, and later that night, I just let it go. I gave myself permission to feel the anger, pain, and sadness. It felt good to just allow myself to feel something other than numb. In addition, it was comforting to know that I was not the only one who had gone through a painful situation, and with time all would be well.

Over time, as I began to really walk in healing, I was able to offer the same support and encouragement to other women who had gone through similar situations. In addition, I was able to share my personal testimony of how God was and is able to restore and mend a broken spirit and heart.

One of the many reasons I desired to be healed was to create a normal, loving environment for my children. I will never forget the night my son, Nicholas, sat down on the couch and said to me, "Mommy, I just feel like my spirit is gone".

Having a four year old child express his feelings in a way that cut to the core of my being was a little too much for me to handle at that moment in time. As a mother, I realized that not only did I have to heal, but I also had to make sure my children healed. Every night after my children went to sleep, I would pray a prayer of restoration, healing, and blessing over them and our house.

We never know the depths or consequences of our choices until we realize that those choices do not just affect us, but the people around us. It is especially devastating when kids are involved and hurt behind some of those choices. The pain children feel is just as deep and real as the hurt an adult endures, however children express and deal with hurt differently. The deep level of hurt that involves the breaking up of a family or loss of a loved one almost seems too much to bear on the heart of a child. They may often act out, or become depressed, increasingly angry, and sad.

My children and their sanity were one of my biggest concerns. I knew that not only did I need help dealing with my pain, but my children needed help as well.

My son, Nicholas, was four years old when his world got turned upside down. He was once a vibrant, curious child, but he became very quiet and un-focused, and started questioning many aspects of life. My youngest daughter, Moriah was too young to remember the chaos and turmoil, yet for some reason, she does remember her lilac room full of color!

As a mother, I had to make sure that both my step-daughter and son knew that our decision to divorce had nothing to do with them. There were many nights when my son would ask why his father lived in one house and we lived in another. I told my son that his father and I made certain choices, some not so good choices, which had nothing to do with him or his sisters. I reassured him that everything would be alright. One thing that my kids could be sure of was they would be taken care of and loved. I assured him that God would always be there with us, loving, protecting, and guiding us along the way.

Those words that I spoke to my son were not only comforting to his ears, but his heart as well.

In so many ways, I could see that the pain that ached in my heart also ached my son's heart. I knew that if I could get on the road to healing, then my kids could get on the road to their healing as well.

So as you sit here reading this, perhaps you realize that while you have been consumed with the hurt and devastation of your situation, so have your children and loved ones close to you. As you demonstrate healing, restoration, strength, and courage, you will give them permission to experience healing and strength too.

The only words that can truly describe the ultimate goal of healing are "Getting Your Joy Back". When you can become alive with life and it begins to take form in your heart, it will start to show in your eyes, words, and smile, and miraculous things will begin to take place in and around you.

A real friend is one who walks in when the rest of
the world walks out.
Walter Winchell

ACTION STEP:
1. Identify a person who has made a difference in your life and let them know how much you appreciate them.

_____

_____

_____

_____

_____

_____

To Forgive Is To Live and Be Free

I can clearly recall the day my ex-husband and I finalized our divorce.   I woke up that morning with a sense of peace, anticipation, and I am not going to lie -"a nervous energy".   I was not sure if my ex would appear in court, but whether he did or did not, I was prepared to finally close that chapter of my life. Sure, we still had two beautiful kids together, but the "tie" would be "formally" severed and I was okay with that part.

The painful process of divorce is something that I would not wish on my worst enemy, but the reality is that it happens. That day, my sister accompanied me to court, and as we sat in there looking around, I began to think about the number of women who had sat in the exact same spot I was sitting in waiting for the judge to appear. I imagine that countless thoughts went through their mind – thinking about how it all came to this, replaying conversations, fights, and tears, and how this will affect the kids, wondering if they will be able to fully recover from the divorce and if they will ever be able to trust and love again. I began to think of women who may have left out of the courtroom completely and utterly bruised, battered and broken, both financially and emotionally, as a result of the divorce. I began to think about the women, who like myself, did not get into marriage believing that one day they would end up a divorced and a single parent - broken mentally, emotionally, and financially. At the same time, I thought of how many women who sat in my exact same spot feeling totally relieved that the process of divorce was soon to be over, and the chapter closed.

It was in that moment that it dawned on me that in order to truly move on with my life, I needed to forgive my ex-husband, release the pain of the past, forgive myself, and let go. We both made mistakes in our marriage and to dwell on the past would only hinder and limit my healing and opportunity to become a better person.

We proceeded with the hearing and it took all of five minutes for the judge to give her "speech", for our lawyers to "concur, we reviewed the divorce decree, concurred with all that was set in the order, the judge pronounced us divorced, case closed, and we were free to go.

As I left the courtroom and walked toward the elevator, I asked my ex-husband if I could talk with him for a moment. I explained to him that even though we did not work out, I wished him well, I forgave him for all the past hurt, and I hoped that he could forgive me as well. In that moment, there was a strong feeling of relief, peace, and closure. It was if a huge weight had been lifted off my shoulders and liberty had taken over. It was wonderful! It was almost as if I had taken all of the power that I had given over to one man back.

Better, not bitter, was what I wanted. *The World English Dictionary* defines forgiveness as the act of forgiving or the state of being forgiven or the willingness to forgive. To forgive is to "grant pardon of an offense, debt" or my favorite, "to cease to feel resentment against". Forgiveness is by far the most important step in the process of rebuilding your life.

In The Bible, Peter asks Jesus how many times he should forgive his brother whom has sinned against him, and Jesus replies that he should forgive seventy times seven (Matthew 18:21-22), which basically means there is no limit to the number of times we should forgive.

It can be extremely difficult for some people to forgive and completely move on without feeling resentment or bitterness. Our natural response is to become angry, bitter, and shut down. Forgiveness is not just for the other person however, but it is for you. Forgiveness is an opportunity for you to release inner feelings of resentment and pain and to move on.

Any thoughts or acts of forgiveness must be based on a conscious effort and a conscious choice. To choose not to forgive is making the choice to hold on to anger, resentment, and bitterness, which ultimately eats at your soul.

In one of Marianne Williamson's works, *A Return to Love*, she describes a meditation exercise which involves visualizing yourself as a child and taking yourself back to a time in your childhood when you felt lost and scared, and then you having to forgive and comfort yourself. This is such a powerful exercise. I remember one night sitting in my room, closing my eyes, and visualizing myself as a child around 12 years old, curled up beside the dresser and crying hysterically. I remember this because it was the same night I called a teen hotline just longing to speak to someone who would listen. During that age, I felt so down and depressed about life and myself. I remember talking to the young woman on the other line and telling her that I felt ugly and alone. As I looked at the little girl on the phone, I bent down and told her how much I loved her and that everything was going to be alright. These are words that I rarely remember hearing during this time of my life and it was during this time that I longed to hear them the most.

As my eyes opened and the tears streamed down my face, I felt a sense of peace and love over-take my entire body. I believe a part of my heart healed tremendously by doing the exercise and offering love and forgiveness to myself as a little girl.

As you embark on this journey and make the conscious decision to forgive yourself and those around you, make a conscious decision to take yourself back to the place of when you first felt that point of hurt and pain. You may have been a young child or teenager, or a young adult. Offer forgiveness to yourself and allow the warmth of God's unconditional love to consume you in that moment in time.

> *The weak can never forgive. Forgiveness is the*
> *attribute of the strong.*
> Mahatma Gandhi

Trust The Process

Trust that once you have handed the circumstance and situation over to God, forgiven yourself, and forgiven the people who may have hurt you, YOU will begin to feel much better, lighter, and free. This is not to say there will not be moments where it seems like you are going backwards, or things will be smooth. There will be moments and situations that arise that may test your patience and strength, but if you keep steadfast and believe for the very best, all will be okay. Look at every situation as a blessing and learning experience.

The Power of Tears

Have you ever felt an enormous sense of joy, love, comfort, and peace that caused tears to begin to overflow in your heart and down your face? Tears are an expression of not only sadness, but joy. Think of the birth of a newborn child or the experience of unconditional love and thankfulness that you feel for your partner or loved one. Better still, think about the powerful love of God in you and around you...sometimes when we stop and think about all of the good, it overtakes us emotionally and brings us to tears.

Angela O. Bryce

There is sacredness in tears. They are not the mark of weakness, but of power. They speak more eloquently than ten thousand tongues. They are messengers of overwhelming grief...and unspeakable love.
Author Unknown

Once you believe in yourself and see your soul as divine and precious, you will automatically become a being who can create a miracle.
Dr. Wayne Dyer

It Takes Courage

*Courage doesn't always roar. Sometimes courage is the quiet **voice** at the end of the day saying, "I will try again tomorrow.*
Mary Anne Radmacher

Out With The Old & In With The New

What if you had a choice between keeping your favorite pair of jeans that fit you as snug as a glove, or trading them in for a brand new pair of dark denims blue j's (my own word for jeans ☺) that seem to lift your butt and accentuate curves in all the right places? What would you do? Would you keep the worn, comfortable pair, or take a chance and give the dark baby j's a try?

Many of us would stick with what is familiar and comfortable to us, even though we feel and look fabulous in the new pair of jeans! We need to be redeemed from the old and in with the new.

Redemption is being free from the past and liberated to think, do, be, and become all that God has created you to be. Redemption stirs the spirit and anchors the soul. It makes no sense to stay in the same state because of familiarity.

Being redeemed is a step on the way to freeing yourself, and being free is to live fully to the extent of which you were created: free from limitations, free from inhibitions, and free to be who you are capable of being. Allow yourself the freedom to do just that and do not be afraid of what others may say, think, or even do.

Blossom and Bloom

Every one of us will go through a wilderness experience at one time or another in our lives, however we may not all encounter the same wilderness experience. My wilderness experience and wake-up call involved the dissolution of a marriage and what I once thought was the "ideal family". It was during this process of heartache, humiliation, and emotional distress that I discovered my true self and realized who I was and was to become. It was there in the wilderness that I faced all of my inner demons from my past, and truly realized that only a living, breathing, and loving God continuously loves, cares, lives and breathes in and through me.

I do not regret the experience because it is during this road that I discovered and learned valuable life lessons about myself and my life. It was in the wilderness that I blossomed, bloomed, and the very core of my being was healed. For this, I am grateful.

There will be distractions along the way. The kids may start acting up, household appliances may start acting funny, finances may start acting funny, and your boss may start acting crazy. All of these "distractions" will come up and in the process, you may get derailed and off track for a little while.
How do you get back on course?

First and foremost, become aware of what is going on inside and all around you. Also realize that the temporary "craziness" is only a distraction and it will pass. Secondly, "Breathe" deeply and fully. We breathe to center ourselves and bring ourselves back into alignment with our being, and when we do, everything is alright. Third, Pray. Prayer brings our connection back to God and the Divine Holy Spirit. Lastly, "Remember Thank You". If we take a moment and look back to where we were in the past to where we are today, then we will clearly see that we have come a long way. Be thankful for where and who you are today. Thank God for the many blessings in your life and the many blessings to come. Remember that things are getting better for you.

What you do not want is to become so consumed by the distraction or challenges in your life that you forget that your current situation or circumstance is only temporary. You have to believe in your heart of hearts and soul of souls that whatever may be a challenge right now will not last forever. There is nothing more heartbreaking than to look up one day and realize that life has passed you by and you missed it because you were distracted by the circumstances of life events. The dreams and desires that once used to wake you up at night will begin to only seem like a distant memory and faded dreams.

Continue with the process of refining your mind, spirit, and soul. Let God be your strength and let him be your guide. Allow the joy and light that lies within you to shine bright for the world to see. Do this in spite of circumstances and challenges, because it all shall pass.

When you were born, what if you were told that you were made in the exact image of God, one with Him, and had complete access to God's everlasting goodness? What if you were told that you were born innocent, pure, and good through God's atonement and resurrection with Jesus? What if you were told that this world we live in is filled with abundant peace, joy, and love?

We do not live in a world of "What Ifs" and many of us did not grow up being told that we were made in the image of God, perfect and filled with His Spirit. Many of us came from an environment which was far from perfect; many of us have gone through some things and made some bad choices, gone down some roads that have caused us to question who we are. Yet through all the imperfect mess, flaws, and "crazy" choices we have made, we are still standing and living in the goodness of God's love and strength.

Every day we get up, we write a story of our lives and it is up to us to create and mold it any way that we desire. As I grow older and find myself opening up my heart, mind, and body to new possibilities, my preconceived notions of how I view life, love, and spirituality are changing, and it is changing for the better.

There is a new-found meaning to the words "I am God's child". There is power in the words "I abide in Him and He abides in me".

As a spiritual being and woman of strength, love, courage, and peace, take hold of these words and let them resonate in YOUR spirit. This process is about a re-birth of mind, body, and spirit for the better. For one second, minute, or hour of the day, open your heart, mind, and spirit to new possibilities for yourself and life. It is YOURS for the asking and it all begins with you. Say "Yes" to your magnificence. Say "Yes" to all the goodness that God has for you and called you to be. Lastly, say "Yes" to love, "Yes" to loving you, and a resounding "Yes" to life.

Chapter 5: Better*Sweet*

By sharing my story, it is my sincere intention that you are encouraged and inspired to move forward, transform, and rebuild your life for the better from the inside out. I have learned that transformation is a journey and process. In addition, rebuilding from the inside out, is an everyday commitment and choice.

From the moment you open your eyes, choose to be better than you were the day before. Let your heart fill up with gratitude, and self-love for simply being who you are, right where you are. I have learned that in every choice that you make, it is either made out of love, confidence, and power, or based on fear, limitations, low self- esteem, and doubt. Begin today by making choices that create peace, love, and joy on the inside. Begin today, living, breathing, and knowing that God desires and wants the very best for you, which is why He created you in His image. Choose today to be Better*Sweet*! :-)

Better*Sweet*

Appendix: Personal Thoughts Journal

Use this section to write and express your thoughts and feelings, and also choose this moment to forgive, let go, and move forward.

_____

_____

_____

_____

_____

_____

_____

_____

_____

_____

_____

_____

_____

_____

_____

_____

_____

_____

_____

_____

Better*Sweet*

Personal Thoughts Journal

Angela O. Bryce

Personal Thoughts Journal

Personal Thoughts Journal

Personal Thoughts Journal

_____

_____

_____

_____

_____

_____

_____

_____

_____

_____

_____

_____

_____

_____

_____

_____

_____

_____

_____

_____

_____

_____

_____

_____

Personal Thoughts Journal

Angela O. Bryce

Personal Thoughts Journal

_____
_____
_____
_____
_____
_____
_____
_____
_____
_____
_____
_____
_____
_____
_____
_____
_____
_____
_____
_____
_____
_____
_____
_____
_____
_____
_____

Personal Thoughts Journal

Angela O. Bryce

Personal Thoughts Journal

_____

_____

_____

_____

_____

_____

_____

_____

_____

_____

_____

_____

_____

_____

_____

_____

_____

_____

_____

_____

_____

_____

_____

Personal Thoughts Journal

_____

_____

_____

_____

_____

_____

_____

_____

_____

_____

_____

_____

_____

_____

_____

_____

_____

_____

_____

_____

_____

_____

_____

_____

_____

_____

_____

_____

_____

Angela O. Bryce

Personal Thoughts Journal

Personal Thoughts Journal

Angela O. Bryce

Personal Thoughts Journal

_____

_____

_____

_____

_____

_____

_____

_____

_____

_____

_____

_____

_____

_____

_____

_____

_____

_____

_____

_____

_____

_____

_____

_____

_____

_____

_____

_____

Personal Thoughts Journal

Angela O. Bryce

Personal Thoughts Journal

Personal Thoughts Journal

Angela O. Bryce

About the Author

Angela Bryce is a visionary, leader, businesswoman, writer, creator, speaker, and Founder of Lady In Balance LLC. More than seven years ago, Angela began hosting interactive workshops and publishing inspirational newsletters and articles encouraging women to have hope, strength, and determination to fulfill their dreams and be all that they desire to be in life. More importantly, Angela chose to say "Yes" to life, "Yes" to self-love, "Yes" to healing, and "Yes" to being all that she was and is called to be. With a background in Psychology, a Master's in Business with an emphasis on Management, Certifications in Coaching and Bodyflow, and a knack for connecting with people from all walks of life, Angela brings a free-flowing, bright light to the area of balance in mind, body, and spirit.

Angela understands and knows the importance of maintaining balance and taking time to nourish the mind, body, and spirit, which is essential and an absolute necessity for women to move forward, heal, and blossom. Angela wholeheartedly gives honor and praise to God for continually keeping, covering, and blessing her to evolve, transform, and become the woman He designed her to be in this life. Angela resides in Northern Virginia with her husband and children.

About Kingdom Journey Press

Kingdom Journey Press, Inc. is a full-service publishing company specializing in providing customized services to support our clients from the conception of an idea to getting HIStory to the masses! Since the time of inception and in conjunction with our umbrella organization, Kingdom Journey Enterprises, we have become recognized globally for our ability to establish a unique presence, while building relationships with partners and clients consisting of current and aspiring writers, and ministry, business, and community organizations.

Our services include:

- ❖ Manuscript Evaluation
- ❖ Coaching for current and aspiring authors
- ❖ Editing
- ❖ Cover and Print Layout Design
- ❖ Print and E-Book Format
- ❖ Copyright and Distribution
- ❖ Marketing and Sales Support

To contact us and to learn more information about our services, we invite you to visit our website at www.kjpressinc.com.

CPSIA information can be obtained at www.ICGtesting.com
Printed in the USA
BVOW02s1357270813

329569BV00001B/2/P